LARRY ULRICH
ARIZONA
MAGNIFICENT WILDERNESS

PHOTOGRAPHY BY LARRY ULRICH

WESTCLIFFE PUBLISHERS, INC. ENGLEWOOD, COLORADO

CONTENTS

International Standard Book Number:
ISBN 0-929969-66-9
Library of Congress Catalogue Card Number:
86-051593
Copyright, Photographs and Text: Larry and
Donna Ulrich, 1987
Book designer: Gerald Miller Simpson/Denver
Typographer: Edward A. Nies
Printed in Korea by Sung In Printing Co., Ltd.
Seoul
Published by Westcliffe Publishers, Inc.
2650 S. Zuni Street
Englewood, Colorado 80150-1261

*First frontispiece: Morning light illuminates sandstone
buttes, Monument Valley Navajo Tribal Park*

*Second frontispiece: A late-winter snowfall blankets
the Great Mojave Wall, as seen from The Abyss,
Grand Canyon National Park*

*Third frontispiece: The walls of Marble Canyon
reflect in the Colorado River below Badger Rapid,
Grand Canyon National Park*

*Title page: Ponderosa pines on the edge of
Rocky Prairie, White Mountains*

*Right: A Sabino Canyon cactus garden is witness
to a clearing storm, Santa Catalina Mountains*

PREFACE

We're roadrunners. We travel Arizona's highways, backroads, and trails . . . searching, searching. We're not looking for food, as the feathered roadrunner does, but for photographic images — nourishment of a different sort. Up and down the mountains, deserts, and waterways we travel, wondering what the next turn will reveal, always expecting the unexpected.

Arizona is a land of infinite design: the extraordinary, almost bizarre landforms; the down-on-your-belly details; the color and the light. It is a landscape that cannot be viewed casually. It is no more possible to walk up to the rim of the Grand Canyon for the first time and not be stunned than it is to cross the border from California into Arizona and not be aware that the landscape is dominated by a galaxy of ungainly cacti called the saguaro. Neither is it possible to walk through the prehistoric Indian ruins at Betatakin without thinking of the Anasazi who once dwelled there. In Arizona, the threads of human and geologic history intertwine, making travel here more like travel in a time machine than in any place we've been before.

This is a state whose geologic, or Earth, history is diverse. Written on the canyon walls and hidden in the desert sands are clues to the origins of this landscape. If you can read between the layers of rock, you will learn their stories. The stories are of ancient sea beds and petrified sand dunes, of periodic episodes of volcanic activity and continuous cycles of deposition and erosion. Nowhere is the Earth history more evident than in the Grand Canyon. During a 20-day boat trip down the Colorado River, we drifted past canyon rocks that were two billion years in the making, the secrets locked within the stratified layers sometimes revealing themselves to us: ancient lizard-like tracks, frozen in stone; milky-white travertine formations, through which flowed Windex-colored water; Vishnu schist, the oldest rock in the canyon, sculpted and mirror-polished by nothing more than the river and time.

The human history of Arizona tells a story, too. Occupation of the desert Southwest has been continuous for more than 10,000 years. Rich and varied cultures still exist today in tribes such as the Apache, Hopi, Navajo, and Papago. The influence of Spanish explorers is also evident in customs, place-names, and architecture.

Learning about some of the state's geologic and human history, as well as its plant and animal communities, has helped us actually see more. While Larry rarely photographs wildlife, we have learned from the creatures that have creatively adapted to their environment: the lizard that somehow speeds across hot sand as though jet-propelled; the coatimundi, with its secretive, nocturnal ways; and the ubiquitous roadrunner — ever searching, every watchful. As with our critter friends, we, too, try to see beyond the obvious.

We've become familiar with Arizona's light. The way the light reacts with the landscape is what makes this state so photogenic. It can be the warm, glowing light of the canyons. It can be the dazzling, uncut light peculiar to the high mountains and the Mogollon Rim. Or it can be the searing, hot light of the desert — the kind that challenges the optics of any lens. It's all special. Every photograph leads to the next, and with each shutter release we get more than an image on emulsion — we also get stories.

And how we love to tell the stories! One of our favorites recalls the time we found Harquahala Valley covered with at least 100 acres of poppies. It was an incredible spectacle of gold. Larry

Snow engulfs a stand of ponderosa pines,
Grand Canyon National Park

photographed the extravaganza all afternoon, into the evening, and again the next morning. Image after image of poppies and owl clover, poppies and lupines, poppies and saguaros, poppies and more poppies. As we were preparing to leave, we noticed a large flock of sheep moving into the area. We wondered what changes the woolly army would bring about. Curious, we decided to return. Only three days had gone by, but what a transformation. The hooved locusts had eaten or trampled every single flower. Where once had lain a carpet of gold there was now little more than an ugly, munched-up land. We're still thankful that we got there first.

To those who suggest that our lifestyle is glamourous, we tell the story of the flash flood we encountered while photographing Seven Falls in Bear Canyon. That's where I discovered that waist-high water on a six-foot-two-inch man is considerably less threatening than on a five-foot-two-inch woman. And even though one stood well above the waters and the other gulped her way along, we both had to hike many miles while soaking wet from head to foot. All for a photograph. Is that glamourous?

At Keet Seel, the largest and best-preserved of Arizona's Anasazi villages, we experienced a violent July thunderstorm. As we watched the lightning from our vantage point inside the ruin, we wondered if the Anasazi would have momentarily stopped their work to watch a storm such as this. It was an incredible display. The rain fell in torrents. The thunder echoed strangely, as though contorted. Across the river, the slickrock — always true to its name — gathered, funneled, and dispersed the rain, turning the deluge into watery exclamation points that thundered off the canyon walls. And then, just as we thought it couldn't rain any harder, it did. The water flew off the lip of our alcove, cascading in a wide veil 20 feet in front of us. When the storm had passed and the rain had ended, we picked our way carefully through the many rivulets that braided the sandbars between Keet Seel and our campsite. Later that night, the moon rose in a clear sky, lighting the ghostly vestiges of a civilization long gone, and we wondered again about the people who had inhabited this canyon for a mere 50 years.

The photographs in this book are the result of such stories, and many more. En masse, they take you on a visual journey through Arizona's wild landscape. We hope you are as surprised as we were at the diversity of this state. You will find that it is not the arid wasteland many envision. Clear mountain streams, full of trout, flow through pine-covered ranges. The desert, Arizona's incredible centerpiece, can change from an inhospitable place to an inviting wonderland awash with springtime wildflowers. And snow-capped peaks, ringed with maples and aspen, reveal autumn color that rivals any New England display.

Arizona's landscape, and its people, are woven together like the strands of a Navajo rug. Red, green, and blue; earth, water, and sky. The colors and patterns repeat themselves in myriad combinations, all blended to perfection. We're lucky. Our work here will never be done. There will be no final sweep of the loom nor last knot to tie. For us, there will always be more scenery to photograph and words to write. Ours is a quest that will last a lifetime. Little wonder in a state whose ambiance is so powerfully woven. We hope you agree.

Donna Bacon Ulrich

Indian paintbrush nestles under petrified sand dunes, Paria Canyon-Vermilion Cliffs Wilderness

COLOR

That we can see at all is amazing; that our vision is blessed with color is a miracle. Color photographers are drawn instinctively toward bright colors, but the subtlety of color is what sustains us. In nature, the most beautiful colors are those that surprise our senses with their quiet tones and vibrant clarity. Our world is a vast symphony of light, seasoned liberally with color.

The banks of Oak Creek covered with autumn color, Oak Creek Canyon

Overleaf: Sneezeweed and ox-eye daisies dominate a meadow along the West Fork of the Black River, White Mountains

Keet Seel ruin, Navajo National Monument

Cathedral Rock looms above Oak Creek,
near the town of Sedona

Mexican poppies and owl's-clover blanket the desert floor,
Organ Pipe Cactus National Monument

Havasu Creek tumbles over travertine formations,
Grand Canyon National Park

Winter tightens its grip on the West Fork of the
Little Colorado River, White Mountains

The lush surroundings of Vassey's Paradise are
formed by springs bursting from redwall limestone above
the Colorado River, Grand Canyon National Park

After a rainy spring, brittlebush blooms in profusion
in the Puerto Blanco Mountains,
Organ Pipe Cactus National Monument

Quaking aspen in Long Canyon, White Mountains

Overleaf: Saguaros silhouetted at sunset,
Saguaro National Monument

*The graceful canary columbine brightens the dark recesses
of Hell Hole, Aravaipa Canyon Wilderness*

*Windows eroded in Navajo sandstone,
Canyon de Chelly National Monument*

A contrast in blooms — Englemann's hedgehog,
Sonoran desert; and sneezeweed, White Mountains

*Honey bees, frozen from a cool evening, still cling to a
Rocky Mountain beeplant, Navajo National Monument*

*Barrel cactus and teddy bear cholla below Palm Canyon,
Kofa National Wildlife Refuge*

FORM

Imagination is triggered by forms in nature: an unusual geologic formation, the contrast between color and texture, the sensuous swirl of a sandstone wall. These manifestations of our environment send the photographic eye careening off canyon walls or reveling in a sea of snow-covered branches. It is a journey of endless possibilities.

Navajo sandstone designs, Arizona Strip

Overleaf: The eroded forms of Coal Canyon catch the morning light, Navajo Indian Reservation

Jimsonweed along Antelope Creek,
Navajo Indian Reservation

A giant saguaro cactus rises to meet the clouds,
Buckskin Mountains

*An Arizona sycamore frames Cathedral Rock above
Cave Creek, Chiricahua Mountains*

*A slot canyon along Antelope Creek gives evidence of
water's erosive power, Navajo Indian Reservation*

*Overleaf: The last leaves of autumn succumb to winter in
the aspen groves above Williams Valley, White Mountains*

Palm Canyon harbors Arizona's only grove of native
California fan palms, Kofa National Wildlife Refuge

White House Ruin,
Canyon de Chelly National Monument

The Skull Eyes stare stoically from their perch above
Cave Creek, Chiricahua Mountains

Arizona sycamore leaf nestles among agave spines,
Galiuro Mountains

*Volcanic activity is responsible for many of the prominent
features in Arizona's landscape — Sunset Crater,
Sunset Crater National Monument; and welded tuff
columns, Chiricahua National Monument*

Balanced rocks below the Vermilion Cliffs,
near Lees Ferry

Petrified logs, remnants of a once-vast forest,
Petrified Forest National Park

Manifestations of winter — naked branches of
the Arizona alder, Secret Mountain Wilderness; and
snow-covered sage, Grand Canyon National Park

Dissolved limestone creates bizarre travertine formations,
Tonto Natural Bridge

Autumn-colored aspen line Hart Prairie,
San Francisco Peaks

MOMENT

"Moment" represents the gamble that is inherent to photography. It is the chance of place, timing, weather, perception, and technique . . . the breaking of a storm, the last light of day sneaking between clouds, the discharge of a million volts of electricity on a faraway butte. Though elusive, these moments can be predicted intuitively. When they're preserved on film, the gamble pays off.

The last light of day highlights petrified logs in Jasper Forest, Petrified Forest National Park

Overleaf: A frosty meadow thaws slowly in the not-so-warm sun, White Mountains

*The fury of a summer thunderstorm strikes over the
Mitten Buttes, Monument Valley Navajo Tribal Park*

*San Pedro Valley stretches toward the Galiuro Mountains,
Santa Catalina Mountains*

Saguaro cactus and the Ajo Mountains,
Organ Pipe Cactus National Monument

Sunset Crater from Bonito Park,
Coconino National Forest

Overleaf: From Toroweap Overlook, the
last light of day flashes over the Colorado River,
Grand Canyon National Park

*Dew-covered spiderwebs glisten in the morning light in
the Black River country, White Mountains*

*Cochise Head from Heart of the Rocks,
Chiricahua National Monument*

Thunderclouds loom over Crescent Lake,
White Mountains

Vishnu Temple and the San Francisco Peaks from
Cape Royal, Grand Canyon National Park

Overleaf: Moonset and sunrise over the
San Francisco Peaks, Bonito Park

SOFT LIGHT

When a day set aside for photographing the landscape is filled with soft light, look closely. This special lighting is better suited for intimate scenes than for grand panoramas. Subjects that you would normally walk past or step upon are most appealing. Soft light is mellow and diffuse, deeply saturated and free of heavy shadow. I never pass up a chance to photograph during a soft-light day.

Aspen enjoy a summer rain over the Kaibab Plateau, Grand Canyon National Park

Scarlet sage clings tenaciously to a rock face,
Aravaipa Canyon Wilderness

Forest ablaze with bright leaves of bigtooth maples,
West Fork of Oak Creek Canyon

A summer storm brings freshness to foliage lining the
banks of the Black River, White Mountains

The polished surface of two-billion-year-old Vishnu schist
defines the course of Monument Creek
as it makes its way toward the Colorado River,
Grand Canyon National Park

Overleaf: Quaking aspen wear a dusting of snow,
Coconino National Forest

Showy asters hide beneath foliage, Oak Creek Canyon

The delicate winding mariposa
tulip contrasts sharply with weathered rocks,
Lake Mead National Recreation Area

*Gambel oaks rise out of bracken ferns on the
Mogollon Rim, Coconino National Forest*

*Hardy blooms get a firm grip on the volcanic soil
of a cinder cone, Sunset Crater National Monument*

Flood waters tumble over large boulders in
Virgus Canyon, Aravaipa Canyon Wilderness

New sedge shoots sprout from their old rootstocks,
Oak Creek

PLACE

I've done my job as a photographer if I can convince viewers that they have been there before, or at least think they have. If I succeed in giving my audience a sense of place, then it doesn't really matter if they have been there or not. What matters is that they feel a personal involvement and can appreciate the beauty of the scene.

Evening light reflects in the Colorado River at the mouth of Monument Creek, Grand Canyon National Park

Ethereal light fills Matkatamiba Canyon,
Grand Canyon National Park

Mojave mound cactus above South Cove,
Lake Mead National Recreation Area

Overleaf: Coconino sandstone formations,
Mogollon Rim

*A cluster of saguaro cactus buds await their
time to bloom, Superstition Mountains*

*The headwaters of the Little Colorado River,
Mount Baldy Wilderness*

Utah juniper stands guard over Maricopa Point,
Grand Canyon National Park

The West Fork of Oak Creek,
Secret Mountain Wilderness

Overleaf: The Little Colorado River nears its confluence
with the Colorado River, Grand Canyon National Park

Teddy bear cholla and ocotillo, Superstition Wilderness

Swollen by heavy rains, Seven Falls roars through
Bear Canyon, Pusch Ridge Wilderness

INFINITY AND
MICROCOSM

Photographers have the freedom to determine how they will portray the world. On some days, when the eye is drawn inward, only close-ups will do. Other days, the eye is continually drawn toward the horizon, and it is grand scenes that must be photographed. Balancing these two artistic desires is a constant sensual struggle — to focus on infinity, or to drop to your knees and examine the world at your feet.

Petroglyphs raise more questions than they answer, Saguaro National Monument

*Moods of the desert spring: Englemann's prickly
pear cactus, Grand Canyon National Park; and Mexican
poppies under Saddle Mountain, Harquahala Valley*

Bear Wallow Canyon from Schnebly Hill,
above Oak Creek Canyon

A ponderosa pine cone is nearly lost in a jumble of leaves
on forest floor, Chiricahua Wilderness

Overleaf: Aspen leaves dot fresh snow, Inner Basin,
San Francisco Peaks

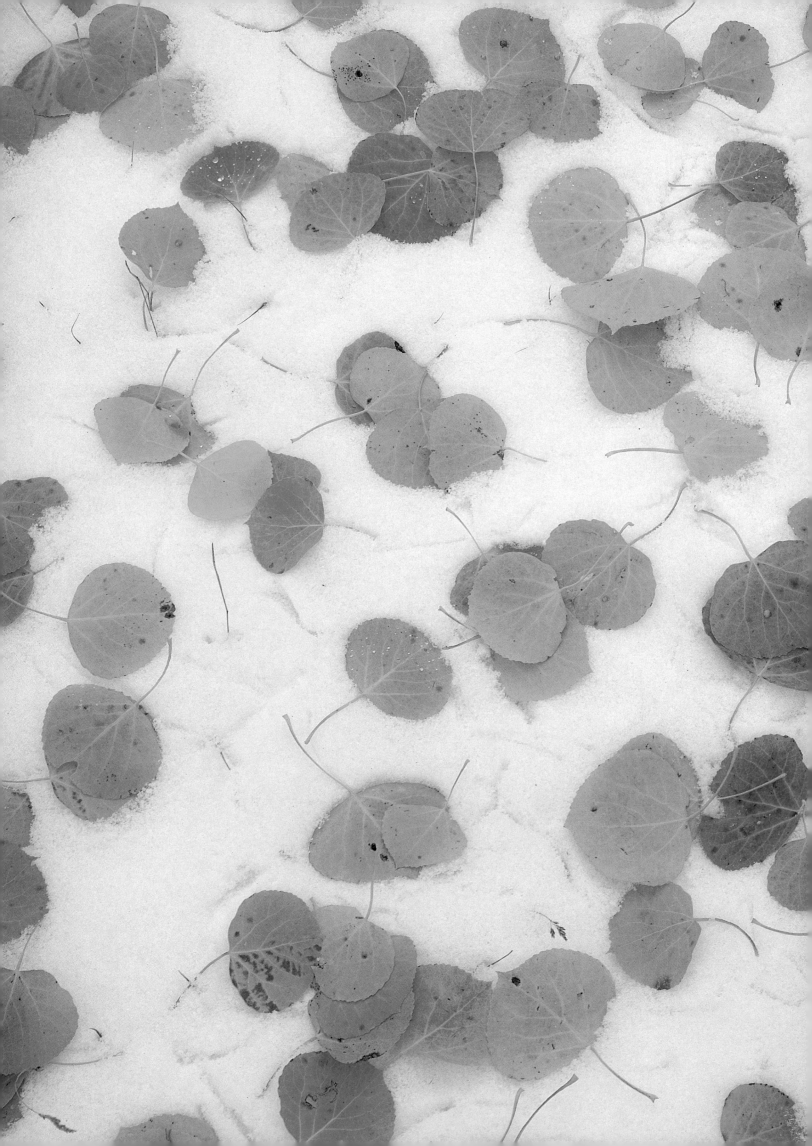

The sun-baked plates of the desert tortoise shell surrender
to the elements, Organ Pipe Cactus National Monument

Maidenhair ferns in winter, Pajarita Wilderness

The mystical Amanita muscaria can be found growing in
the White Mountains, Mount Baldy Wilderness

Pedestal logs on Blue Mesa,
Petrified Forest National Park

Overleaf: The Mitten Buttes guard
Monument Valley during summer thunderstorm,
Monument Valley Navajo Tribal Park

TECHNICAL
INFORMATION

The photographs within this book were made with an Arca Swiss 4 × 5 view camera, occasionally employing a Horseman 120 format film back. Lenses used were in focal lengths of 75mm, 90mm, 135mm, 180mm, 250mm, and 360mm.

Kodak Ektachrome 64 professional transparency sheet film was used exclusively. Polarizing filters were used in direct light situations to reduce glare from the surface of natural objects. An 81B warming filter was used in cloudy conditions to correct for the blue cast of Ektachrome film. Red filters, 10CC and 20CC, were used to correct for reciprocity failure of the film during long exposures. Exposures were calculated with both a Pentax 1-degree spot meter for reflected light, and a Gossen Luna-lux meter to calculate incidental light.

The film transparencies were separated on state-of-the-art laser scanning devices by the printer. Color reproduction was achieved with the goal of duplicating on paper the scene as it appeared to the photographer at the moment the image was made.

Evening comes to Marble Canyon on the Colorado River, Grand Canyon National Park